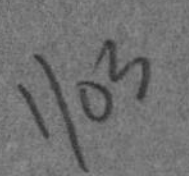

SANTA CRUZ CITY CO
D0478536

Loon Summer

For Michael, Beth, and Laura.
Also, for the Rainy Lake Gang and Jane Yolen.
— B. S.

For Emmett and Amanda. I love and cherish you.
— A. S.

Published 2001 by Eerdmans Books for Young Readers
An imprint of Wm. B. Eerdmans Publishing Co.
255 Jefferson Ave. SE
Grand Rapids, Michigan 49503
P.O. Box 103, Cambridge CB3 9PU U.K.
www.eerdmans.com/youngreaders

Printed in Hong Kong
01 02 03 04 05 06 07 7 6 5 4 3 2 1

Library of Congress Cataloging-in-Publication Data
Santucci, Barbara.
Loon summer / written by Barbara Santucci ; illustrated by Andrea Shine.
p.cm.
Summary: While spending the summer with her father, Rainie wished her
parents would stay together, just like the family of loons she sees on the lake.
ISBN 0-8028-5182-7
[1. Divorce–Fiction. 2. Fathers and daughters–Fiction. 3. Loons–Fiction. 4. Birds–Fiction.]
I. Shine, Andrea, ill. II. Title.
PZ7.S23863 Lo 2001
[Fic]–dc21
00-055097

The illustrations were rendered in watercolors and cut paper.
The text type was set in Venetian.

Loon Summer

Written by **Barbara Santucci**  *Illustrated by* **Andrea Shine**

EERDMANS BOOKS FOR YOUNG READERS

GRAND RAPIDS, MICHIGAN / CAMBRIDGE, U. K.

My first morning at the lake, sunshine peeks through the blinds and warms my face. Then I hear the loons.

"Oh-OOOO-oooo."

Their sad songs remind me Mom isn't coming to the cottage this summer. I turn my face away from the sun.

"Rainie," Dad calls out. "Come see. The loons are back. Hurry!"

I rub sleep from my eyes and throw on my clothes. Dad and I head for the cove. Two loons soar above us, then land near the reeds that hug the shore.

Dad and I hide in the brush. We watch the loons rush across the water and stretch out their wings to take flight.

"Oh-OOOOO-oooo."

"You told me loons stay together for life," I say. "Why can't you and Mom?"

Dad's mouth gets a twisty kind of look that means he's upset. "Things change, Rainie. But you and I will always spend summers at the lake together."

"It's different now," I say.

"Some parts will be the same," says Dad, reaching out to hug me.

The next few mornings, I watch the loons collect twigs and brush for their nest. I sit on the greening grass and weave violets into necklaces.

"Loon necklaces," Mom always called them. I place the chain of violets over my head, like she always did. The tiny flowers tickle my neck. Tears tickle my eyes.

One afternoon I sit on a hill overlooking the lake and search for the loons' nest. Dad comes and sits beside me, then hands me his binoculars. I look through them and finally spy the nest in the reeds.

"I see two eggs, Dad." I point to the nest near the edge of the cove. "They're a real family, just like we used to be."

"We're still a real family, Rainie."

"Not like the loons."

Dad doesn't answer.

On hot days, Dad and I float on rafts.

I slide off into the water. "Race you!" I shout.

Dad comes after me.

We dog-paddle to the dock and climb up on it, then turn around and jump back into the lake.

When I pop up, I spot the loons. Two gray chicks are riding on their parents' backs. I wrap my arms around Dad and ride piggyback too.

As the loons grow bigger, they swim side by side — like Dad and me. We watch them dip their heads underwater. Fishing, the loon way.

Many mornings Dad and I paddle quietly to the cove. Dad baits our hooks, then we drop our lines side by side. Fishing, our way.

One day Dad hands a worm to me. "Now bait your own hook, Rainie."

The worm slips from my fingers.

"Mom always put the worm on for me."

Dad just smiles.

Finally, a worm stays on the hook. I smile back at Dad.

Some days we pick blueberries along the shore. Mom always made jam for us out of the berries. Now Dad and I eat them right off the bushes while we walk. They still taste sweet.

One afternoon we sit and watch the young loons learn to swim underwater. We hold our breath until they pop up, farther and farther away.

"I want to do that, too." I tell Dad. "But I'm scared."

"We'll practice," says Dad.

Every day I try swimming underwater. First just one stroke, then two, then three. Pretty soon I can swim underwater almost as far as a loon chick looking for fish.

When I pop up, Dad is always there.

Our time at the cottage goes by fast. I want to go home to the city and be with Mom. I want to be at the lake with Dad. I want things to be the way they used to be.

But I know they can't.

Our last night at the cottage, Dad and I warm our toes by the campfire. "Whoever finds the North Star makes the first wish," he says. Dad always lets me win, but this time I want him to. So I let him find the North Star.

"Tell me your wish," I say.

"My wish is that you'll never forget how much Mom and I both love you. Even when one of us isn't with you."

I snuggle close to Dad. He kisses the top of my head.

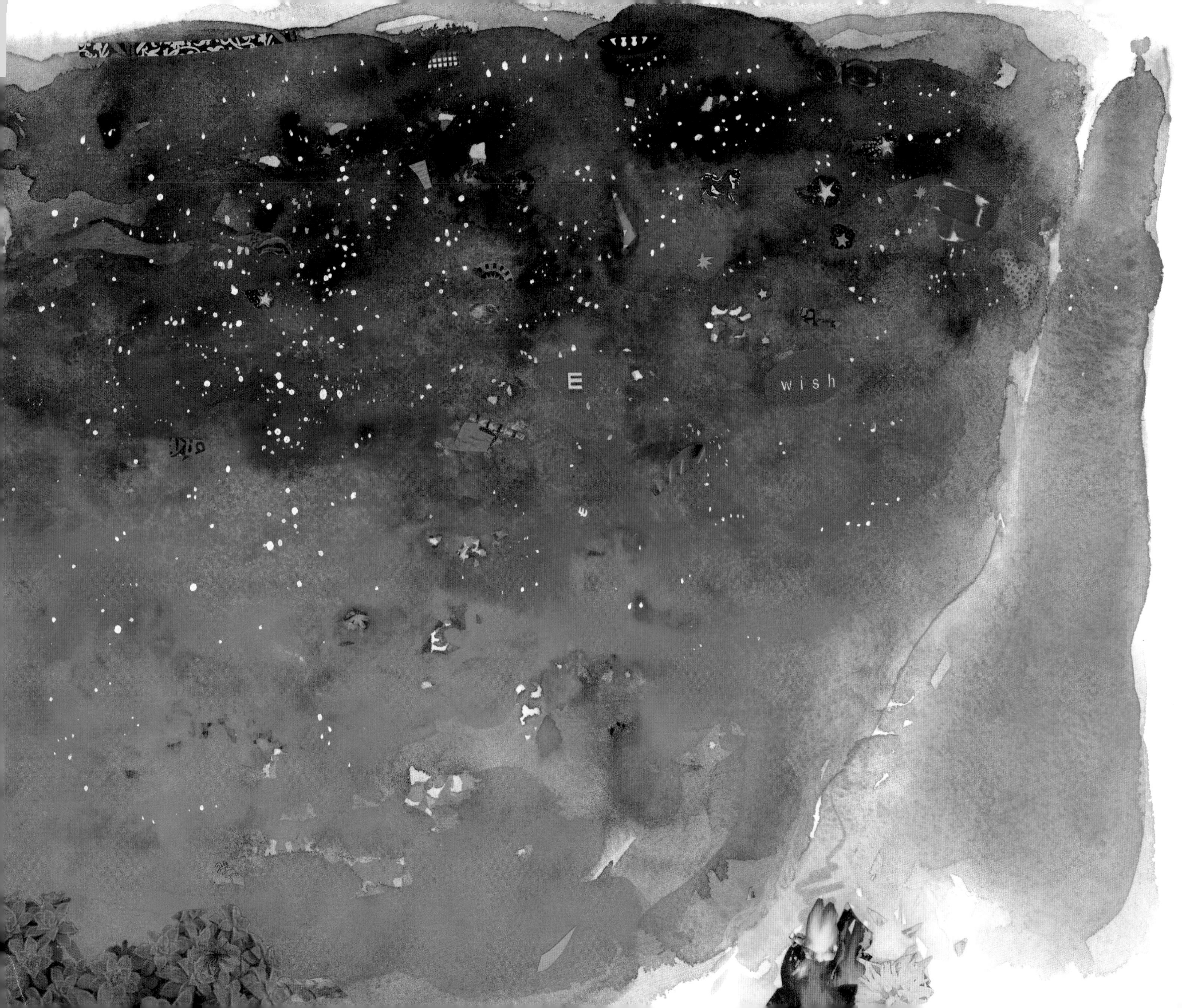
E
wish

PLANTS

The next day as we pack to leave, our loon family joins a flock of other loons that gathered on the lake. In a rush of flapping wings, they all start to fly away.

"Oh-OOOOO-oooo," they call.

"Oh-OOOOO-oooo," I call back. "I'll miss you." I turn to look at Dad.

The loons fly higher and higher with their necks stretched south.
I wave goodbye knowing they will return next summer.

pocket

Just like Dad. Just like me.